Ducks

Baby Animals™

ALICE TWINE

PowerKiDS press™

New York

For two dapper gents, Binkleton Puddleduck III and C. Colin Brinkman

Published in 2008 by The Rosen Publishing Group, Inc.
29 East 21st Street, New York, NY 10010

Copyright © 2008 by The Rosen Publishing Group, Inc.

First Edition

Editor: Amelie von Zumbusch
Book Design: Julio Gil

Photo Credits: All images © Shutterstock.com.

Library of Congress Cataloging-in-Publication Data

Twine, Alice.
  Ducks / Alice Twine. — 1st ed.
     p. cm. — (Baby animals)
  ISBN-13: 978-1-4042-3771-1 (library binding)
  ISBN-10: 1-4042-3771-2 (library binding)
  1. Ducklings—Juvenile literature. I. Title.
  QL696.A52T85 2008
  598.4'1139—dc22
                                                2006037225

Manufactured in the United States of America.

Contents

What Is a Duckling?   4

Kinds of Ducklings   10

A Duckling's Life   16

Words to Know   24

Index   24

Web Sites   24

A baby duck is called a duckling. A duckling's **feathers** are softer and fuzzier than an adult duck's feathers.

All ducklings have a **bill**.
Ducklings breathe, eat, and
drink with their bills.

Ducklings also have **webbed feet**. These webbed feet help ducklings swim. Ducklings are good swimmers.

There are many kinds of ducklings. This duckling is a mallard. Mallards live all over the world.

Some ducklings, such as this Pekin duckling, live on farms. Pekin ducklings are yellow.

13

Muscovy ducklings also live on farms. When they grow up, these ducklings will have a red spot near their eyes.

Mother ducks lay eggs in a nest. After several weeks ducklings will hatch, or break out of the eggs.

17

Ducklings learn to swim the same day they hatch. When they are young, ducklings swim close to their mother.

Ducklings drink water. They eat many different things, such as bugs and plants.

21

This is a mother duck with **juveniles**. Juveniles are ducklings that are growing up but are not yet adult ducks.

23

Words to Know

bill

feathers

juveniles

webbed foot

Index

B

bill(s), 6

F

feathers, 4

J

juveniles, 22

W

webbed feet, 8

Web Sites

Due to the changing nature of Internet links, PowerKids Press has developed an online list of Web sites related to the subject of this book. This site is updated regularly. Please use this link to access the list:
www.powerkidslinks.com/baby/ducks/